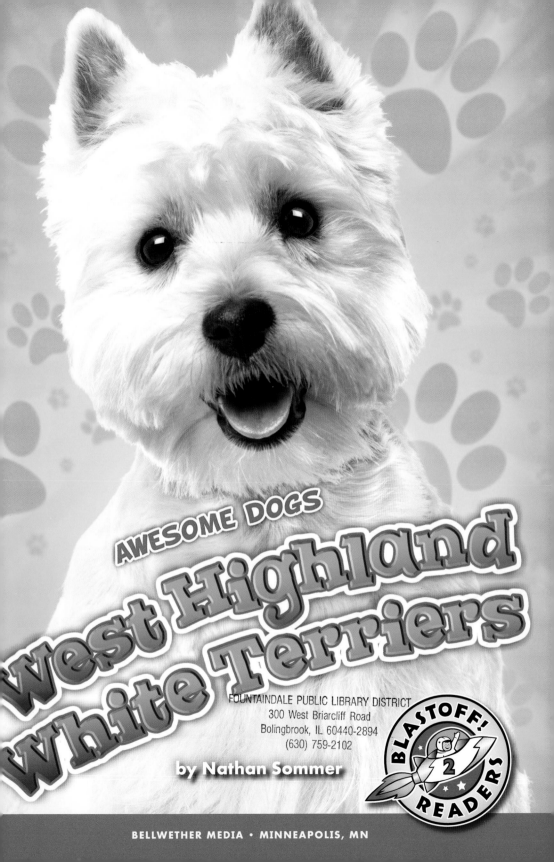

AWESOME DOGS

West Highland White Terriers

by Nathan Sommer

BLASTOFF! READERS
2

BELLWETHER MEDIA • MINNEAPOLIS, MN

Note to Librarians, Teachers, and Parents:

Blastoff! Readers are carefully developed by literacy experts and combine standards-based content with developmentally appropriate text.

Level 1 provides the most support through repetition of high-frequency words, light text, predictable sentence patterns, and strong visual support.

Level 2 offers early readers a bit more challenge through varied simple sentences, increased text load, and less repetition of high-frequency words.

Level 3 advances early-fluent readers toward fluency through increased text and concept load, less reliance on visuals, longer sentences, and more literary language.

Level 4 builds reading stamina by providing more text per page, increased use of punctuation, greater variation in sentence patterns, and increasingly challenging vocabulary.

Level 5 encourages children to move from "learning to read" to "reading to learn" by providing even more text, varied writing styles, and less familiar topics.

Whichever book is right for your reader, Blastoff! Readers are the perfect books to build confidence and encourage a love of reading that will last a lifetime!

This edition first published in 2018 by Bellwether Media, Inc.

No part of this publication may be reproduced in whole or in part without written permission of the publisher. For information regarding permission, write to Bellwether Media, Inc., Attention: Permissions Department, 5357 Penn Avenue South, Minneapolis, MN 55419.

Library of Congress Cataloging-in-Publication Data

Names: Sommer, Nathan, author.
Title: West Highland White Terriers / by Nathan Sommer.
Description: Minneapolis, MN : Bellwether Media, Inc., [2018] | Series:
  Blastoff! Readers. Awesome Dogs | Audience: Age 5-8. | Audience: K to
  grade 3. | Includes bibliographical references and index.
Identifiers: LCCN 2016052740 (print) | LCCN 2017013857 (ebook) | ISBN
  9781626176164 (hardcover : alk. paper) | ISBN 9781681033464 (ebook)
Subjects: LCSH: West Highland white terrier–Juvenile literature.
Classification: LCC SF429.W4 (ebook) | LCC SF429.W4 S66 2018 (print) | DDC
  636.755–dc23
LC record available at https://lccn.loc.gov/2016052740

Editor: Betsy Rathburn   Designer: Kathy Petelinsek

Printed in the United States of America, North Mankato, MN.

Table of Contents

What Are West Highland
   White Terriers?   4

Dogs of One Color   8

History of West Highland 12
   White Terriers

Lots of Energy   18

Glossary   22

To Learn More   23

Index   24

West Highland white terriers are a fun-loving dog **breed**. They are energetic and love to be social.

The dogs are often
called Westies.

Westies have **sturdy** little bodies. They can weigh up to 22 pounds (10 kilograms).

They have deep chests
and muscular legs.

Dogs of One Color

All Westies have white fur.
They have thick double **coats**.

The outer coats are rough.
Beneath are short, furry
undercoats.

Westies have dark, almond-shaped
eyes. Pointy ears stick up on
their heads.

West Highland White Terrier Profile

pointy ears —

dark eyes

carrot-shaped tail

Life Span: 12 to 20 years

Trainability:

1 2 3 4 5 6

Hardest to train   Easiest to train

Some people say their tails look like carrots!

History of West Highland White Terriers

Westies were first born in Scotland. There, they were used as hunting dogs.

Scotland

N
W E
S

They were especially good
at catching small animals.

No one knows why Westies are white. Some believe they were **bred** that way on purpose.

They say hunters did not want to confuse the dogs with other animals.

The **American Kennel Club** first included the breed in 1908. The dogs are in its **Terrier Group**.

Today, Westies are loved
by many pet owners!

Lots of Energy

Westies are active and **alert**. These **independent** dogs are always ready for adventure.

They love to explore and dig
in their backyards!

Westies get along with everyone.
They are friendly with children
and strangers.

These bold dogs enjoy playing with their families!

Glossary

alert—quick to notice or act

American Kennel Club—an organization that keeps track of dog breeds in the United States

bred—purposely mated two dogs to make puppies with certain qualities

breed—a type of dog

coats—the hair or fur covering some animals

independent—able and willing to do things alone

sturdy—strongly built

Terrier Group—a group of dog breeds originally bred for hunting mice and other small animals

undercoats—layers of short, soft hair or fur that keep some dog breeds warm

To Learn More

AT THE LIBRARY

Gagne, Tammy. *West Highlands, Scotties, and Other Terriers*. North Mankato, Minn.: Capstone Press, 2017.

Petrie, Kristin. *West Highland White Terriers*. Minneapolis, Minn.: ABDO Publishing Company, 2014.

Schuh, Mari. *Yorkshire Terriers*. Minneapolis, Minn.: Bellwether Media, 2016.

ON THE WEB

Learning more about West Highland white terriers is as easy as 1, 2, 3.

1. Go to www.factsurfer.com.

2. Enter "West Highland white terriers" into the search box.

3. Click the "Surf" button and you will see a list of related web sites.

With factsurfer.com, finding more information is just a click away.

Index

adventure, 18

American Kennel
  Club, 16

backyards, 19

bodies, 6

bred, 14

breed, 4, 16

chests, 7

children, 20

coats, 8, 9

color, 8, 14

dig, 19

ears, 10, 11

explore, 19

eyes, 10, 11

families, 21

fur, 8

heads, 10

hunting, 12, 13, 15

legs, 7

life span, 11

nickname, 5

owners, 17

Scotland, 12

size, 6

strangers, 20

tails, 11

Terrier Group, 16

trainability, 11

undercoats, 9

The images in this book are reproduced through the courtesy of: Eric Isselee, front cover, pp. 5, 11, 12; C S Wimsey/ Alamy, pp. 4-5; anetapics, p. 6; Mark Raycroft/ Minden Pictures/ Newscom, p. 7; Johan_R, p. 8; Juniors Bildarchiv GmbH/ Alamy, p. 9; Szeno, p. 10; Be Good, p. 13; Waldemar Dabrowski, pp. 14-15; GROSSEMY VANESSA/ Alamy, p. 15; Mirko Graul, p. 16; Lopolo, p. 17; Tierfotoagentur/ B. Mielewczyk/ Age Fotostock, p. 18; Juniors Bildarchiv/ Age Fotostock, p. 19; Salima Senyavskaya, pp. 20-21; Vladislav Gajic, p. 21.